CUSTOM BEETLE

CUSTOM BEETLE

Mike Key

ISBN 1 85532 463 6

Project Editor Shaun Barrington
Editor Simon McAuslane
Page design Paul Kime/Ward Peacock
Partnership

Printed and bound in Hong Kong
Produced by Mandarin Offset

ACKNOWLEDGEMENTS

I would like to take this opportunity to thank all those who helped me in obtaining the photographs for this book. All the owners of the hot bugs in this book, from the U.S.A., Great Britain, France, Germany, Switzerland, Belgium and Denmark, making it as international as possible. Without you guys building the cars this book would not have been possible.

Gene Berg for his help when we were in California.

Reflections of Norwich for the processing of the rolls of film.

VW Trends magazine for the Bill Schwimmer and Ted and Jason Stevens photographs, R.K. Smith, *Hot VWs* magazine for the Bill Newton, Baja and Sean Cour photographs. All the other photographs were taken by myself, using a Nikon FA and range of Nikon lenses.

A special thank you to FUJI for supplying the 100ASA transparency film, which records the superb colour that all of these cars so richly deserve.

Right
A new term for decorative paint over the last few years has been "graphics". This term has been used for anything that has had a row of coloured lines added to the bottom of the car body, to big splashes and to a large curved, wiggly thick line of paint that run the full length of the car; sometimes even onto the side windows. The graphics on this bug have been painted over two or three or more stages.

For a catalogue of all books published by Osprey Automotive
please write to:

**The Marketing Department, Reed Consumer Books,
1st Floor, Michelin House, 81 Fulham Road, London SW3 6RB**

Introduction

This is not going to be a book on the history of the Beetle. If you want that sort of information read something like *Classic Volkswagens* by Colin Burnham. This is a book devoted to VWs which are 'hot'. I have tried to show in the photos that, as well as being hot, these bugs are also highly individual; fun to build and even more fun to drive! I hope I have selected the cars that show the best taste in design and paint of interiors and engines; not only the sparkle but also the horsepower.

I also wanted to collect features from several countries, to make it a truly international book. There are hot bugs from the USA, U.K., France, Belgium, Denmark and Switzerland and not forgetting Germany; without them building the VW beetle, this book would not have been possible.

While in California collecting features for *Custom Beetle*, I was in touch with Gene Berg and his son Gary, who over a period of nine years have put together a '67 Bug. This car was in 1979 driven to the Bug-in 22 and with the addition of a set of slick tyres, stinger exhaust and removal of the fan belt. He then ran an ET of 12.40 at 106.46 mph, which goes to prove that street cars *can* be fast.

A bad accident was the start of a complete rebuild, starting with a good floor pan with new trans mounts welded on it and powder-coated black gloss. A stock ball joint front end was narrowed and modified by Gary. This gave extra tyre clearance and the car's low stance. The rear end is height adjustable and has better stopping power due to the 356 Porsche brakes. With the body on the new and straight floor pan, Dave Triplett of Huntington Beach took care of the body work and sprayed the Manurva blue. This car seemed a great way to introduce the following celebration of Bug metamorphosis.

Contents

HOT BUGS

Right

Gary's bug looks great in the California sun; the stance is just right, the BRM wheels are magnesium originals, very sought after and very expensive. Notice the '67 has one-piece windows and de-chromed trim. I like the bumpers! They're American spec with towel rail overriders. The rear of the car is just as nice, with 185x15 rear tyres on BRM wheels, original rear lights and American spec bumpers.

Below

This is where the 'hot' part of this car comes in; the 2110cc engine has an 82mm Gene Berg forged crank, Carrillo rods, 90.5mm Cima pistons and barrels, Engle FK-87 cam and 30mm Berg oil pump. It also has Clyde Berg modified dual port heads, Berg 1.45:1 rocker arms and a pair of 48IDA Webers on Scat Trak manifolds, with Berg linkage and a Stinger electronic ignition system.

BUG FILE

Owner **Gary Berg**
Body **Mods de-chromed**
Year **1967**
Wheel & tyres front **BRM 155x15**
Wheels & tyres rear **BRM 185x15**
Front suspension **3" lowered spindles**
Rear suspension **Sway-a-way spring
    plates**
Engine **2110cc**
Cam shaft **Engle FK-87**
Ignition **Stinger system**
Carbs **Dual 48mm Weber ida**
Exhaust **Berg 1¾" custom**

A full roll cage was constructed for safety. A pair of Scat Pro Car front seats were equipped with Audi lap belts and upholstered to match the rest of the interior in grey vinyl and cloth. Darker grey carpets go from the fire wall to the front. There is a LeCarra steering wheel, a Berg locking shifter with a Hurst Line Loc, impressive stereo AM/FM cassette system and a huge AutoMeter tach.

Above

Wheels are widened stock VW, with the centres that Peter made with fake Allen head bolts and Wolfsburg centre crests. The door mirrors were made with a combination of milled ally and original arms. The bug sits right from every angle; it has a low, purposeful stance.

Right

Built in a similar style to Gary's car but thousands of miles apart in Germany, this bug was built as a full-on street racer. Peter Voss from Wuppertal built it over a period of two years in his spare time. This is one of those super cars that looks the part and has the performance to match. During the building of this car, Peter came up with ideas of his own to make it a very personal bug: the stock '74 1300 was purchased locally and the rebuild started with the body being split from the floor pan. At the front of the pan is a fully loaded front beam with Sway-a-way adjusters, urethane brushes and a heavy-duty anti-roll bar. A Porsche 356 C gear box was bolted up in the rear with Type 3 rear drums to increase the stopping power. With the floor pan complete it was time to turn the attention to the body, which has hints of Cal-look about it, very similar to Gary Berg's. These are: the de-chroming of the exterior, the removal of the bonnet and engine-lid handles, door handles and bumpers are colour keyed with the front indicators from a Golf set into the front bumper. Peter chose to use fibreglass wings for the front and rear, with the old-type sloping headlights. Smooth window rubbers and a radical louvred deck lid with a pope's nose number plate light completes the exterior look. Pete did all the paint work himself.

Under the bonnet, Peter built the battery box in the spare wheel well. The fuel tank is chrome-plated and has fitted hinges so as to ease access to the steering, fuel pump and brake master cylinder. It also gives the viewer a taste of the finish to the bug. The bumper at the front is "floating" as Peter puts it. There are no holes in the front valance; the brackets come from underneath the valance.

Looks like a Type Four conversion, but it's not! This engine is based on a Type One case with a Porsche fan conversion (these are very popular in Germany) which provide better cooling. The 1800cc engine has a 69mm counterweighted crank and a hot street cam with lots of headwork, resulting in a pretty hot motor – just what the Germans like. A pair of Italian 44mm Webers push in the juice and a Bosch 009 distributor helps with the fire. It looks clean and business-like.

The hot street look is carried into the interior; you will find no floor mats, just polished ally floor panels. There is no rear seat either, just a rear roll cage finished off in green paint and carpet. In the front Peter bolted in a pair of Recaro seats for that body-hugging fit. The stock dash has been smoothed over and a set of Porsche 911 gauges installed.

BUG FILE

Owner **Peter Voss**	Rear suspension **Stock**
Body mods **De-chromed**	Engine **1800cc**
Year **1974**	Cam shaft **Hot street**
Wheels & tyres front **Widened stock**	Ignition **009**
Wheels & tyres rear **Widened stock**	Carbs **Dual 44mm Webers**
Front suspension **Sway-a-way**	Exhaust **Home-made**

Above

City Sign Services came up with the graphics, which were applied over the Cliff Green paint. This is an original VW colour and it was sprayed on by Andrew Coker. The wheels are split rim Compomotive 3 inch front, 6 inch rear by 15 inches, with polished outers and colour coded centres.

Left

Here we have an English street and strip hot bug. Andy Smith took time out to build this 1972 street racer. With a best 14.01 at 93mph it is no slouch. Like the two previous bugs, it has that race flavour. For ease of work, the rear wings come off on Dzus fasteners and the rear valance drops of in minutes. This helps with the quick removal of the engine; the front end is a one piece tilt. This was as a result of an accident – when Andy came head to head with a tanker – which meant a written off front end. Something had to be done, so Andy cut away the damaged metal and built the one-piece front end himself. Under this is the front end from a 1500, complete with disc brakes and a Select-A-Drop. Also a spun ally tank is mounted on the steel bulkhead. Instead of fitting the original headlights, Andy went for a pair of Cibie Oscars, under which are a pair of small turn indicators. Andy took the race bug over to the French "Super VW" meeting at Jablines. The deck lid has 'Stand Offs'; extended hinges to aid cooling on the way from Calais to Paris.

As you can see from this shot, the rear of the body drops off in minutes, exposing the engine – ideal for working on at race meetings. Bernie Smith of Wagenmaster created this little beauty, using a 78mm Bugpack crank with 8 dowels and 90.5mm barrels and pistons, which equals 2007cc of motor. The Hot cam came from Gene Berg of California, other Berg parts include a oil pump, dual valve springs, retainers, followers and 1.4 forged rockers. A pair of 45mm Dellorto carbs are bolted to Street Eliminator heads. To finish the engine off, a Bugpack exhaust was used. Bernie built a super tough gearbox with hardened keys and a Bugpack Beef-a-Diff.

As with most race-type interiors, it is basic: ally panels and dash, six point roll cage, Luke harnesses, window safety nets, and a fire extinguisher. On the dash are VDO gauges, speedo and large rev counter. This is important if you don't want to blow it up through over-revving.

BUG FILE

Owner **Andrew Smith**
Body mods **De-chromed tilt front**
Year **1972**
Wheels & tyres ft **Split rim compomotive 3x15 125x15**
Wheels & tyres rr **Split rim compomotive 6x15 205/65 vr 15**

Front suspension **Select-a-drop**
Rear suspension **Stock**
Engine **2007cc**
Cam shaft **Gene Berg**
Ignition **009**
Carbs **Dual 45mm Dellortos**
Exhaust **Bugpack**

Left

This is Tom Lubbock's second hot bug. The first was a 1303 with a Turbo body kit. He wanted to build a Cal-looker; a 1970 1300 model had been on one side for some time, the 1303 became tatty, so the engine and the wheels from that went into this project. The Porsche 914 ally replica wheels, with two ear spinners were repolished by Tom, taking around 2 hours each. Before the body could be tackled, the floor pan was painted and restored. Next came the mechanics at both ends, the front beam had Sway-a-ways fitted to give it that low-down stance; Mini shocks by Monroe were fitted to cope with the lower front, drumbrakes were given the once-over. Not to be left out of the lowering, the rear was dropped one spline, with the Porsche wheels mounted on the pan and 145 tyres on the front and 195s on the rear, both 15 inches. It was time to concentrate on the body. Pre-1967 sloping headlight wings are used on the front, the headlights are original metal Rossi units with American custom "Owl Eyes" over the lenses.

Above

De-chroming of the rest of the body went ahead to give it a smooth look. As well as the running boards, the deck lid is completely smooth. Rear lights are 1200 with all red American Spec lenses. Paint is BMW British racing green, two stage pearl, laid on by Andy Bedford, with 12 layers in all, 3 lacquer.

Above

The 1600cc engine from the 1303 was rebuilt, keeping with a standard crank, cam, pistons and rods. Tom took the standard heads and polished and ported them, all chrome tin ware is used and the ignition coil has been moved to the bulkhead. Braided lines and ally dip stick go to make the engine department that more purposeful. 009 dizzy, S&S Rally exhaust and a pair of Baby Dellortos finish the look.

Right

Interior is amazing; the white vinyl-covered Cobra seats in the front and stock rear are particularly striking against the pearlescent paint. As well as the seats, the door panels are also white, as is the centre console and speedo. To finish it off, a four spoke steering wheel – also white. The dashboard has been smoothed. Ally billet winders, handbrake and pedals go well with the rest of the interior. And for that final touch, a 400 watt stereo.

BUG FILE

Owner **Tom Lubbock**
Body mods **De-chromed & smoothed deck lid**
Year **1970**
Wheels & tyres ft **Porsche 914 145x15**
Wheels & tyres rr **Porsche 914 195/65x15**
Front suspension **Sway-a-way**
Rear suspension **1 spline**
Engine **1600cc**
Cam shaft **Std**
Ignition **009**
Carbs **Dual baby Dellortos**
Exhaust **S&S rally**

HOT MOTORS

Left

This must be the neatest hot bug motor I have ever seen! It is fitted in a 1962 cabriolet and belongs to Dan Deering of Colorado. It is a 1904cc with a Turbocharger under the rear valance. This makes for a very neat engine compartment. The engine was built by Dan's brother Scott, who installed all the 'hot' stuff. A 74mm Scat forged crank, 8-doweled, stainless steel rods, 90.5 cylinders and pistons and Engle 120 cam. The carbs are 40mm DRLA Dellortos. Scott also designed the IHI turbo with built-in waste gate, Dan runs about 5lbs of boost which can be adjusted from the dash. The exhaust system was custom-made by Toni Piconi.

Above

German bugs with the familiar Porsche shroud; the Germans like their engines Hot. These two were visiting France at the Super VW meeting just outside Paris. Both cars passed us on the way back to the ferry on the French motorway and they were cruising in the fast lane. Say no more!

Above

Andy Parrott spent a lot of time on his engine bay and, again, neatness is the key to success. The basic machining work was done by Autocavan. Fitting of the dowels, lightening the flywheel and balancing the pistons were done at night school by Andy. The 1641cc engine has a standard balanced crank, 87mm pistons, Euro-race cam, 009 dizzy and a pair of Dellorto DRLA 40 carbs. As you can see there is much detailing in billet aluminium; these parts were made by Andy on a manual machine. He produced such parts as the dizzy cover, dipstick, pulley nut cover and oil filler head. However, the carb air filter tops were done on a CNC milling machine. Fan housing has been smoothed and painted the body colour.

Right

This hot motor is in a French owned bug. It is a good example of how to make a stock engine look very neat. He has used chrome tin ware and a chrome 30 horsepower fan housing. The engine is complemented by the polished louvred fire-wall and sides. Body colour has been used on the dizzy cap, spring and solenoid and it looks just right.

BUG FILE

Owner **Chris Newsham**
Body mods **D&D specialties roadster**
Year **1961 convertible**
Wheels & tyres ft **Centreline champ 400**
Wheels & tyres rr **Centreline champ 400**
Front suspension **Sway-a-way & Jatech
    dropped spindles**

Rear suspension **Lowered 1 spline 71 IRS**
Engine **1600cc**
Cam shaft **Std**
Ignition **009**
Carbs **Dual 34 ICT Webers**
Exhaust

Rodbuster; if you are into hot rods as well as hot bugs then this is for you. It is influenced by the Ford 32 hi-boy. It was designed by D&D Specialties in Van Buren, Arkansas. Denny and Dale Johns completed most of the work, then sold it to Terry Maheuron who moved it to the east coast to finish it. The fenderless street rod look was Denny's idea and it is based on a 1971 floor pan and running gear. The pan was detailed and the under paint job is as good as that on the body. The front beam is a JC Performance with Sway-a-way adjusters and Jatech forged dropped spindles with Columbia disc brakes. The rear transaxle is a '71 IRS unit which has been lowered by one spline, and contains Bilstein coil over shocks and a set of Columbia disc brakes. Both front and rear suspension has been chromed. To complete the rolling pan, Centreline Champ 400 wheels are used. The body is from a '61 convertible, which has had all the exterior chrome removed and the door handles. Work then started on hammering the body. As you can imagine making the trunk as a one-piece unit was a major task of bodywork, as well as reworking the inner fender. The door sills were also reworked to achieve that clean hi-boy look, these are rolled over the edge of the floor pan by 3 inches. The doors were rehung suicide style, on '55 Chevy hidden hinges. The factory top was replaced with a Carson lift off top, which is held in place by three seat belt latches and takes just minutes to remove. The windscreen was chopped five-and-a half inches and the straight edge along the top is a billet ally caping which is very neat. All the side glass was removed, roadster-style, and the old window slots in the doors and rear quarters capped off.

Above

The rear valance was trimmed up and remoulded using part of the rear wings to give a smoother look, the deck lid was smoothed and number plate frenched in and then punched with louvres, in the Hot Rod style. The rear lights are in a stainless tube with ally brackets almost like a '32 Ford spreadbar and D&D Specialties also shot the lipstick red Deltron enamel paint.

Above right

The engine is all VW! It is a 1600cc stock unit with a smooth 36hp fan housing, chrome valve covers, 009 dizzy and a pair of 34 ICT Webers. A billet ally fan mount and pulley with various anodised fittings and braided line complete the engine bay. To keep things really tidy, all wires are hidden with the exception of the spark leads through the fan housing. Transmission is a stock unit shifted by Hurst Gear Change.

Right

Smoothed-out dash with just the speedo and radio. You can see the neat capping over the chopped windscreen. Ally mirrors on both the doors and a square ally mirror on a small bracket attached to the dash. The seats are from a Pontiac Fiero with speakers in the headrests – they are trimmed in cloth with matching door panels, and the carpet is from a Mercedes. Rodbuster is now in England and is owned by Chris Newsham of Yorkshire.

BUG FILE

Owner **Paul Gibson**
Body mods **Gibson roadster, tilt front**
Year **1967**
Wheels & tyres ft **8 spoke Empi 135x15**
Wheels & tyres rr **8 spoke Empi 195/65x15**
Front suspension **Sway-a-way**

Rear suspension **Stock**
Engine **1600cc**
Cam shaft **Std**
Carb **Single 32/36 Weber**
Exhaust **Extractor**

Roadsters are usually found in California or other hot parts of the USA, but they have also become very popular in Europe. Paul Gibson of Birmingham, England, has been into VWs for some time, owning a Squareback and a Beetle – both modified and both quality cars built on a budget, keeping down the cost. He started this project as part street, part strip racer. The base of the roadster was a rotten '67, which had no bonnet or deck lid and no wings. The whole bottom half was rotten but this was no problem as Paul was going to carry out major Beetle surgery. It was over onto the roof as eventually this was not going to be used. The floor pan was repaired in the battery area and the rear quarters where they had been eaten away by the inner wings. The heater channels were replaced with a 2 inch box which led to the idea of channelling the front end of the body over the floor pan. Paul likes his cars low but also likes the ride of the stock suspension travel; the front bulkhead and the base of the door pillars were cut away to achieve the channelling. One problem did arise; the steering column was now in between Paul's knees. This problem was solved by using a bus column and adding 2 inches in from the Type One giving 4 inches extra, and it was rerouted over the bulkhead to achieve the correct height. A one-piece glass tilt front was made by Bob Elliott, which hinges on a frame at the front that also holds the Citroen Diane headlights and turn indicators so the front tilts and leaves the lights behind. This solves the problem of disconnecting the wires when taking the front off. Under the front is an ally tank that supplies the engine through an SU electric pump.

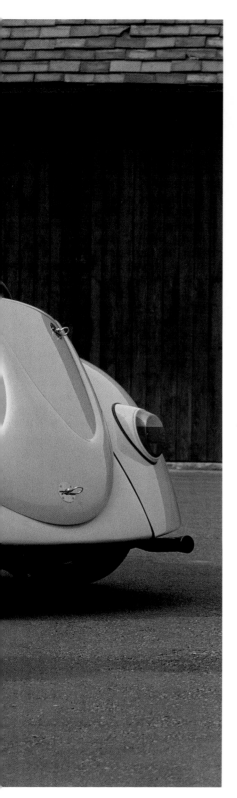

With the roof chopped off it was time to chop the windscreen to a suitable height and cap the ends with shaped ally plates. The doors and rear quarters were capped off with sheet steel and part of the curves from the door tops. A full roll cage made out of one-and-five-eighth inch seamless pipe, which was bent by Paul with a rented pipe bender. The six point roll cage is welded to the chassis rails at the front and centre and to the steel plates at the firewall. With all the weight taken off it was found that, even with the channelling, it still sat high and a pair of Sway-a-ways soon brought it down to the correct height. Silver Empis contrast well with the Volkswagen rally yellow paint. The deck lid and smooth running boards were also made by Bob out of glass.

Above

The 1600 twin port motor is stock bar for the single progressive Weber carb and a set of 1.4 ratio rockers. The engine bay is super-clean and fan housing is smooth with no heater ducts. A hot 1800cc will be used for racing.

Right

Interior is also clever; a pair of bucket seats of unknown origin replace the front seats and are covered in white vinyl. There is no rear seat, but a steel frame covered with ally forms a storage area. Door and rear quarters are ally panels and the dash is smoothed out with just the speedometer and switches showing. Note how the channelling is done in the door sill.

This roadster is a bit more unusual than the others. One look will tell you there are no doors. These have been welded shut and also the interior panels are steel; this simplified construction. First Kevin of Basildon, Essex, took a standard 1967 sedan, cut off the top, leaving the windscreen pillars to the height required. He then set about smoothing the whole of the exterior, welding the doors shut and blending the front and rear wings into the body. The deck lid was cut to the right shape and it was welded onto the rear valance, with the engine obtaining its cooling from the large hole in the deck lid. The top half of what was the body and where the grille was could now be welded and smoothed over. Kevin then smoothed out the rest of the top edge. He also thought it would be a hot thing to just panel the inside of where the doors were. He could then paint the whole of the smoothed exterior and the interior. Not to leave anything out, he gave the dashboard the smoothing treatment too, just leaving the speedo. A pair of Porsche front seats and the standard rear were covered in white. A wood Mountney steering wheel completes the interior, bar the serious stereo system and two sub-woofers in the rear.

41

BUG FILE

Owner **Kevin Hood**	Rear suspension **2 splines**
Body mods **Hood roadster**	Engine **1200cc**
Year **1967**	Cam **Std**
Wheels & tyres ft **Empi 8 spoke 135x15**	Ignition **Std**
Wheels & tyres rr **Empi 8 spoke 165x15**	Carbs **Std**
Front suspension **Lowered**	Exhaust **Stinger**

Above

Paint is diamond white with fluorescent pink, Hawaiian metallic blue and straight pink at the front. Wheels are Empi 8 spoke and are colour keyed fluorescent pink at the rear and metallic blue at the front. They carry 135x15 front tyres and 165x15 on the rear. One item on the roadster that is not welded to the body is the trunk lid but this opens forwards instead of lifting up in the stock manner. The front was lowered by playing around with the front bed; MG metro shocks were also used on the front. The rear was lowered by two splines. The front lights are stock early Beetle.

Right

Kevin left the engine stock, which is a 1200cc. This has been painted to match the rest of the body, and a Stinger exhaust system was installed for more horsepower and some throaty noise. The engine bay is also smoothed out and painted with the same graphics. The rear lights are teardrops.

BUG FILE

Owner **Luc Caluwaerts**	Front suspension **Dropped 4½"**
Body mods **Wizard roadster, chopped**	Rear suspension **Dropped 3"**
4.5 inches	Engine **1900cc**
Year **1962**	Cam **Engle**
Wheels & tyres ft **Borbet 7x15 Fulda 195x15**	Ignition **009**
Wheels & tyres rr **Borbet 9x16**	Carbs **Dual 44 Webers**
Bridgestone 245x16	Exhaust **S&S four tip**

Left

This must be the lowest in suspension and top for a Wizard roadster. The roadster was built by Luc Caluwaerts of Belgium. Based on a 1962 beetle, Luc started by fitting the roadster kit and then decided to chop the screen by four-and-a-half inches. He remade the top to give the right contours. Front lights are USA spec. Indicators are behind the slotted gills in the front wings, which are also modified – they have been widened by two inches. The rear wings are widened by three inches.

Above

As you can see, the roadster sits very low to the ground, the front has been lowered four-and-a-half inches, and the rear has been lowered three inches. The floor pan has been strengthened and now has an independent rear suspension. It does look good with the tyres tucked up in the wings! On the front are 7x15 Borbet wheels with Fulda tyres and 9x16 on the rear with Bridgestone tyres. Ventilated discs are on all four corners as are Monroe shocks. Colour is sky blue.

Right

Not only did Luc want it low but he also wanted it fast! To this end he built a 1900cc engine, starting with a welded stroker 69mm crankshaft, forged con rods, forged Mahle pistons (94mm), Manley valves 40 and 35.5, on Engle cam and 009 distributor. Cylinder heads have been polished to aid the gas flow of the pair of Weber 44 carbs. The exhaust system is an S&S four tip. Cooling is taken care of by a Porsche shroud, colour keyed to the body and interior paint. Stainless louvred fire wall and tin ware finish the look of the engine bay.

Above

The stock dash has been replaced with an ally panel. This houses the Porsche 911 gauges painted blue, front seats are from a Simca Rally, rear seat was made by Luc; steering wheel is 9 inch Formula one and Scat does the shifting. The buttons and window winders are hi-tec, an 800 watt hi-fi system blasts out cruising tunes from a Roadster compact disc player; two Roadster amps and two Woofers.

HOT INTERIORS

Above

Interiors range from outrageous to simple, and sometimes both work. This convertible bug, a 1303, has been trimmed in blue suede with a gorgeous multicoloured fleck in it. The seats are not 1303, but are of the Recaro style. The dashboard hump has been smoothed out and a set of black and white figured gauges have been installed. The front of the dash is also covered in suede, as are the door panels; a very nice, clean interior.

Right

This is a typical French bug interior. Outrageous in pink and multicolour material, it is a good job he went for the grey on the seat top and back. Paint can also be used to good effect; the steering wheel has been painted two-tone pink and blue, as have the gearstick and knob. The pedals are also pink and covered with material. The dash has been smoothed out and just the speedo and the ignition key are left.

Above

Andy Parrott's '73 interior is on the hi-tec side. The dash has been smoothed over leaving the original glove box. A set of VDO night design gauges replace the originals. The cassette player is sunk into the dash. Recaro seats are re-covered to match the rest of the interior in grey and blue velour. All the ally billet parts were made by Andy. A Grant GT steering wheel in blue leather finishes off the interior.

Right

This is what I call a good interior! It is simple as most of the parts are from the original car. The '54 built by John Humphreys has a red painted 'bat wing' steering wheel. The dash is painted body colour with red accented gauges. Also colour coded are the red leather Recaro seats and door panels. An interesting touch is the doorsill trim in ally. As I said, simple but very nice.

BUG FILE

Owner **Herbert Rausch**
Body mods **De-chromed, split rear window**
Year **1961/1966**
Wheels & tyres ft **Empi 8 spoke 135x15**
Wheels & tyres rr **Empi 8 spoke 165x15**
Front suspension **Sway-a-ways**

Rear **Suspension stock**
Engine **1834cc**
Cam **Not known**
Ignition **009**
Carbs **Dual Dellortos**
Exhaust **S&S**

Well here is a real twist! A Canadian living in Switzerland, building a Cal-look (USA), from the German-built VW, photographed by an Englishman in France. That's six different countries involved here – you cannot say that the custom VW scene is not international! This superb, outrageous pink, fake split rear window was built by Herbert Rausch, with help from all his family. The floor pan is a 1966. The original '66 front beam has been lowered with adjustable Sway-a-ways; the front and rear braking system is also original '66, as is the gearbox. Herbert de-chromed the body and front headlight rims, decided to leave the bumpers chrome, but colour keyed the bumper irons and the inside of the bumpers. Earlier we referred to this as a fake split. This is not quite true – an original steel split window and air intake is welded into the 1961 body with an original 'W' deck lid. Just to make it more interesting, it has a full sunroof to pull back on those sunny Swiss days. Colour keying is the charm of this car. The Empi five spoke wheels with 135x15 on the front and 165x15 on the rear are sprayed with the same pink – mixed and laid on by Herbert. You will also see that the same treatment has been carried out on the pair of side mirrors and the wiper arms and blades. The rear lights are original '56.

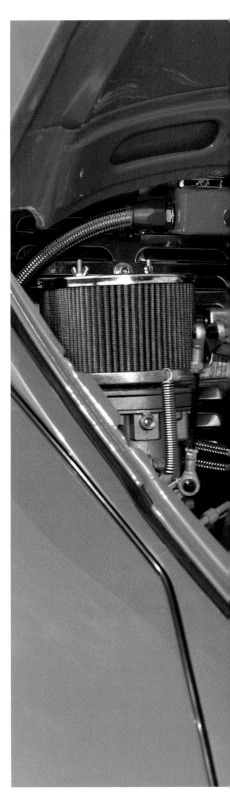

Above

The interior is executed just as well as the rest of the bug. The pink steering wheel, pedals, window winder knobs and escutcheons set off the interior. The dash has been smoothed – leaving the speedo. However, the glove box has been blanked off and houses the radio/cassette player and the petrol gauge. When parked and the glove door is closed, it looks original. The same pinstripe that is drawn down the engine and body side is also across the dash. White leather and cloth cover the original '61 front and rear seats, and also the side panels.

Right

The engine department is a delight. An 1835cc GEX (USA) motor is fitted out with an early fan housing and painted, as is the block, in pink. The pinstripe with a small motif is a copy from the belt line on the body. A pair of Dellorto carbs are fitted for more horsepower. Chroming of the generator and its ancillaries goes a long way to give it the look. Attention to detail on this hot bug is incredible; look into the dizzy cap and you will see the rotor has been painted pink.

Trust the French to come up with something that is novel. Philippe Clay took this stock 1970, 1300 Beetle and set about turning it into something different. In France you are not able to modify the car to any great extent, so with a nip here and there, Phillippe succeeded. The first job was to lower the suspension on the front. The usual method with Sway-a-ways was used. With this goes a pair of short shocks. The rear suspension was lowered by one spline. With this achieved it was time to sort out the body. One-piece windows were installed, the rear large oval VW lights are recessed into the wings and Rossi headlights go into the early front wings, which also hold the front turn indicators. This sunroof 1970 has polished Porsche wheels front (5.5x14) with 145 tyres and rear (5.5x15) with 155 tyres. The detailing of the paintwork needs to be seen. The whole car is covered in yellow motifs and some are in the most unlikely places. As you can see, there are some on the exterior of the body but they have been carried on into the engine bay, steering column, speedo and even into the air intakes placed in the recess at the bottom of the windscreen. The body was in poor shape; it was split from the pan and repaired before being painted white. Philippe, the painter at R.M. Coachworks, a local French company, laid on the fluorescent motifs in yellow and covered these with several coats of lacquer. Philippe also has a T-shirt with the same design on it, and a racing bike too.

BUG FILE

Owner **Philippe Clay**	Rear suspension **1 spline**
Body mods. **De-chromed**	Engine **1300cc**
Year **1970**	Cam **Std**
Wheels & tyres ft **Porsche 5.5x14 145x14**	Ignition **Std**
Wheels & tyres rr Porsche **5.5x15 155x15**	Carb **Std**
Front suspension **Sway-a-way**	Exhaust **Ansa**

Above

The dashboard was smoothed over and in place of the glove compartment are three louvres. The speedo, steering wheel and other parts of the interior have also received the yellow motifs. Philippe's sister had the job of recovering the shortened Audi bench seat and the Audi front seats in a dark grey cloth. The door and side panels were covered in a cloth with fun motifs to go with the paint.

Right

The 1300cc engine is stock with the exception of the Ansa exhaust. But, as you can see, a lot of trouble with paint does give a pleasing effect. The whole bay was first painted white and then the yellow motifs were painted on the fan housing and tin ware. Other engine ancillaries were painted black with splash graphics.

This 1966 Bug was built by Andrew Giles, who purchased it from a retired fireman for £100. The price will lead you to think it was in poor condition and you would be right. When Andrew got down to the basics it was rotten. Rust had eaten into both heater channels, the front bulkhead and all the usual places. A full rebuild of the body panels went ahead and with time the finished body looked excellent. Along the way he decided to de-chrome the side trim, bonnet handle, front indicators and fit one-piece windows and a full-length sunroof. Time was also spent on the floor pan, which was shot blasted and given a good coat of Smoothrite paint to protect it. The front was lowered and a set of 1500 disc brakes was installed. The rear suspension was lowered by one spline and the 1300 gearbox went back in after some detailing. The finished body was reunited with the floor pan and shipped down to S&S Autos of Hunstanton for a Ford peppermint green two-pack paint job.

Above

A 1776cc engine was built by Bernie Smith of Wagenmaster. Gene Berg supplied and prepared such parts as: the 69mm crank rods, 90.5mm barrels, cam shaft, stainless steel valves, (39mm and 32mm) and the rest of the valve train. These were put into the fully reworked (by Bernie) 041 racing heads. Both the oiling and fuel systems are also Berg. The deep sump and oil pump help to cool and lubricate, thus helping in the engine life. 42mm Webers are part of a special Berg kit with fan-mounted linkage. This engine has all the right braided lines and fittings. Early-type fan housing with no heater outlets helps with the clean look.

Right

The interior, by Bernie Newbury of Southend, Essex, is very classy. The front seats are Recaro and have been trimmed with slate grey with light grey panels; the peppermint green piping contrasts with the body colour, and the standard rear seat is covered to match. Door panels were built from scratch and covered in slate grey with a VW logo in peppermint. Door pulls in peppermint compliment the painted winder knobs, escutcheons, pedals, gear stick, steering wheel and handbrake. The dash has also a new layout with the addition of a rev counter, oil temperature and pressure gauges.

BUG FILE

Owner **Andrew Giles**
Body mods . **De-chromed bonnet, shaved, sunroof**
Year **1966**
Wheels & tyres ft **911 Porsche 195x60x15**
Wheels & tyres rr **911 Porsche 195x60x15**
Front suspension **Lowered**
Rear suspension **Lowered**
Engine **1776cc**
Cam **Not known**
Ignition **009**
Carbs **Dual Webers**
Exhaust **Dual Quiet Pack**

BUG FILE

Owner **Glyn Whale**
Body mods, **De-chromed. Suicide doors. Opening windscreen**
Year **1970**
Wheels & tyres ft **356 style .145 Michelins**
Wheels & tyres rr **356 style .145 Michelins**
Front suspension **Sway-a-way**
Rear suspension **Lowered 6 inner splines**
Engine **1200cc**
Cam **Std**
Ignition **009**
Carb **Std**
Exhaust **turbo tuck-a-way**

Above

When you look at Glyn Whale's car with the pop-out 'safari' windscreen, you wonder why Volkswagen did not fit this as an option – it looks perfect! But then the humble Beetle is a people's car. Some custom car builders go for the 'hot in the engine look', some for the hi-tec look, some for the 'cut it up' roadster look. Glyn went for the Cal-look, with some surprises. The Safari windscreen was not easy to fit. Glyn assures us that it was the hardest job on the car. He supplied a pattern to Chris Glover at Brasscraft, who made up the screen using brass channel, which comes apart to replace the glass in the event of an accident and hinges from the centre. It can be removed and the original can be replaced in the winter, as this 'show car' is a daily driver. Other body mods are the de-chrome of the body, no door handles, a smooth deck lid and a bumper-mounted number plate. The indicators have been replaced by flush-mounted VW Passat units, replacing the horn grilles.

Above right

With the removal of the door handles, Glyn also went for hidden hinges to give the Beetle a smooth look. He also reversed the way the doors open – suicide style, and the job was quite involved. It took several attempts to achieve the right fit, eventually coming down to a pair of heavily modified Ford Transit van hinges which adjust in every direction for a perfect fit. A set of Mitsubishi Colt door catches replace the VW ones and the internal door handles still work. Electric deadlocks are 'just in case', as some suicide doors swing open in cornering, hence the name.

Right

Dash has been smoothed but the glove compartment has been retained and the speedo has been repainted old English white with black letters. Seats are Ford XR3 retrimmed in velour and upholstered by Gary Kybert. In every custom there must be some tunes, these are by Kenwood and Pioneer. Paint is by Steve Brown (Exclusive Workshop) and is VW/Audi pearl blue metallic. Exclusive is where Glyn works, and they allowed him to carry out all the bodywork there in his own time.

HOT PAINT

Above
You would have to do something outrageous in the USA Beetle scene to be noticed. This '70s de-chromed bug's smooth running boards, Empi wheels and large bumpers have all been colour keyed in red or white. It certainly must have taken some masking tape to do this job!

Left
Flames, first used on Hot Rods in the USA years ago, usually on black cars, have been adapted over the years into candy colour schemes and onto late model cars as well as rods and customs. They blend well on this Beetle of Carl Klinkenborg's, who designed the flames on a computer, took their pattern and laid them on the Rally Yellow before flaming them in Bizared.

Above

The '69 Mayers Mynx body is on a modified VW Beetle floor pan with the addition of a complete rollcage system. This serves to beef up the Buggy, and with that power unit it is needed. The front suspension is modified VW with disc brakes and Billstein shocks. At the rear is a Carters gearbox with independent suspension, also with disc brakes and Billstein shocks. The Myers Mynx body is painted straight black and this is also the base colour for this roll cage system which is then painted in a splash technique in pink and blue. The buggy rolls on polished centre lines both front and rear, shod with Toyo tyres. Lights both front and rear are after market custom units.

Left

This is one hot beach buggy! The engine was built by Roger Crawford at Heads Up in California USA. The crank shaft is an 84 Scat with Carillo con rods, Auto Craft heads with 38 and 48 stainless steel valves. The eight-and-a half to one compression ratio is fed by a 750 Holley dual feed carb through a Turbo charger and a splash of N.O.S. when needed. To light all this mixture, Mark Philips used a Hay's Stinger EIE ignition system. In the pump department a Berg oil pump was used and for the fuel, a Mallory was used. To blow away this mixture of gases a custom-built S&S header exhaust system was used.

BUG FILE

Owner **Mark Philips**
Body mods **69 Myers Mynx beach buggy body**
Year **1969**
Wheels & tyres front **Centerlines, Toyo tyres**
Wheels & tyres rear **Centerlines, Toyo tyres**
Front suspension **VW modified**
Rear suspension **VW modified**
Cylinder heads **Autocraft**
Ignition **Hay's stinger**
Carbs **Holley 750, injected, turbo and nos**
Exhaust **S&S header custom**

When you ride as a passenger in an open buggy with loads of power, you need something to hold on to! The driver, Mark, has a black Le Carra steering wheel. On the passenger side Mark installed a T-grab handle just for the white knuckle ride. Gauges for the driver include a large rev counter, with red over rev light, a selection of gauges from VDO, head temperature, boost etc. A pair of bucket seats hold you into the cockpit and pink seat harnesses stop you falling out. Behind the seats is the fuel tank, N.O.S. bottle and a fire extinguisher, just in case. There is a cool box for the California heat at the end of a hot bug run in the sun.

Above

It is not often you come across a beach buggy that has the body completely made by the owner. Dirk Tinck from Belgium started with a 1971 floor pan, shortened by 30cm, a lowered front bed and a 1302 gearbox with 1303 suspension. Type Three discs for the front and drums on the rear. Chrome Mangel wheels 7x15 on the front, with BF Goodrich 195/50/15 and 10x15 on the rear with BF 295/50/15 on the rear. With a rolling floor pan the body could now be made. There are three ways to convert this buggy, only the top roof comes off, then the rear part with the rear window comes off to reveal the rear deck with moulded in head mouldings. All these body panels were made by Dirk. The colour is Belgium Touring Security yellow with red metallic flames, headlights are special Buggy units.

Above right

Engine is a 1914cc Type One, giving 120 horsepower. A standard 69mm crankshaft and Mahle pistons make up the short block. Standard 1.6 heads and a pair of IDF 44 Webers make up the top half of the engine. Cooling is by a Porsche 911 fan and fibreglass housing. A Bosch 009 dizzy lights the fire and

a chrome Ansa exhaust system clears the gases. Rear lights are 1967 beetle.

Right

With both the tops off, the handmade dash is revealed within. The two stage dash houses the VDO gauges, kilometers per hour, speedo, rpm, oil pressure, oil temp, cylinder head temp, fuel and clock. A Momo steering wheel helps with directing the buggy and an Empi drag shifter moves it through the gears and provides something to sit on in the form of a pair of Recaro seats from an Opel. A nice, imaginative buggy for all weathers.

BUG FILE	
Owner **Dirk Tinck**	Front suspension **Lowered VW**
Body mods **Buggy home-made**	Rear suspension **1303 VW**
Year **1971**	Engine **1914cc**
Wheels & tyres front **Mangels 7x15 BF Goodrich**	Cam **Engle 110**
	Ignition **Bosch 009**
Wheels & tyres rear **Mangels 10x15 bf Goodrich**	Carbs **Dual Webers IDF 44**
	Exhaust **Chromes Ansa**

BUG FILE

Owner **Adam Tolbot**
Body mods **Gp buggy**
Year **1955**
Wheels & tyres front **Wolfrace 5x15
    Kelly**
Wheels & tyres rear **Wolfrace 8x15 bf
    Goodrich**
Front suspension **Modified VW**
Rear suspension **1971 VW**
Engine **1600cc**
Cam **Stock**
Ignition **009**
Carbs **Dual 34 I.C.T.**
Exhaust **Chrome buggy**

*This ultra-clean, short wheelbase Mark
One G.P. buggy was built by Adam
Tolbot. A joy to drive on a hot sunny day,
this model is the best in open car driving.
The '55 floor pan was shortened by
fifteen-and-three-quarter inches to take
the G.P. body. The front axle and
suspension are chromed and fitted with
two Sway-a-ways. The 1971 gearbox has
the '55 swinging drive shafts and coil
over shocks make up the rear
suspension. Both front and rear brakes
are '55 drums, wheels are 5x15 and
8x15 Wolfrace polished mags. The body
was widened by 2 inches at the rear,
wheel arches and the fronts were flared,
and the side panels were lengthened and
blended into the main body. Bodywork
was done by Adam and friends.*

Above

To show off the very detailed engine, Adam wanted the body to lift up. This is not as easy as it may seem. The body is hinged from the front axle on a homemade hinge, gas rams do the lifting and are mounted at the rear. Adam had to reinforce the body with 20 feet of one-and-a-quarter inch box. The bulkhead to body is strengthened by hidden steel frame work and polished stainless tube. The floor pan is also re-inforced with 1"x1" angle and 2"x1" steel box. This was sprayed in stone chip, primer, paint and lacquer to match the body. The body is painted in cellulose blue metallic base and lacquered. Paint was laid on by Chris and Clive Wright.

Right

A fully chromed engine links to a fully polished and chromed gearbox and trans axle. Adam took the time to hand-polish the gearbox and the engine block. Much work and dedication! A 1600cc engine is basically stock but has twin 34 ICT Weber carbs, 009 dizzy, chrome buggy exhaust and loads of chrome tin ware and braided lines.

BUG FILE

Owner **Bill Newton**	Front suspension **69 adjustable**
Body mods **Beach buggy**	Rear suspension **69 VW stock**
Year **1969**	Engine **125hp**
Wheels & tyres front **Gold strickers Big O**	Cam **N/a**
Big Foot 14x215	Ignition **009**
Wheels & tyres rear **Gold strickers Big O**	Carbs **Dual 48 Dellorto**
Big foot 15x60	Exhaust **Mega duals bug pack**

Right

Engine contains a '74 crank, dual 48 Dellorto carbs, 40/35 valves in the heads, 009 Dizzy, Bug Pack Mega duals for the exhaust system and cranks out 125 horsepower. Rear lights are four Chevrolet Vegas.

Above

The long wheelbase Buggy body is green metal flake impregnated into the gel coat, then the gold panels were painted over and the edge pinstriped. There is also pinstriping over other parts of the body. Dune Buggy headlights, air horns, chrome mirrors and stock VW turn indicators were all part of the scene back then. Mustang seats out of a '66 were covered in green velour by Billy Scot of Louisvillle, who also covered the custom rear seat. Other interior features are the chrome rollbar, Grant steering wheel and Hurst shifter. Dash holds a cluster of Stuart Warner gauges, oil pressure, head temp, amps and rev counter.

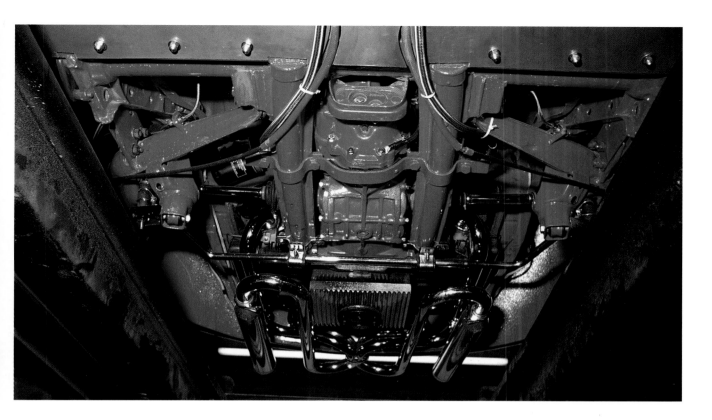

FIRE DOWN BELOW

Above left

Chrome plate has been a favourite for hot rodders for many years. One problem is keeping it clean in wet weather – and I speak from personal experience here. Russell Fielding decided the cleaning chore was not that great a problem, and subsequently had the engine, tin ware, brake drum etc. chromed on his 1969-based Baja bug.

Left

Here is another shot of Andy Parrot's super-clean 1973 Bug. (There is an engine shot under HOT MOTORS.) This car is exceptional in the under parts as well as the outer. An excellent wiring system takes the place of the VW rats' nest. Ally hinges with gas rams replace the tin and spring; ally gas cap and ally disc in the centre of the spare wheel, all neat parts. All the ally parts were made by Andy.

Above

Alan Smart's 1953 is an experience that you do not easily forget. The engine department is hung onto a space-frame chassis with an ally floor. Extra anti-roll bar on the rear, an extra gearbox mount, and a larger sump are just a few extras, and all of these are painted red.

Right

The next three cars featured are all members of the Der Kleiner Panzers (The Little Tanks) a prominent Cal-look club first started in the late sixties in California. The first car, owned by Dave Mason of Elturo, California, is straight out of the mid-'70s. This, I am assured, is how it was – straight paint, such as black, dark green or red, not the pastel colours and wild graphics we have come to look upon as Cal-look in Europe at this time, but more like the German cars. Dave spends time tuning the engine on his 1962 ragtop sedan. It is a 2175cc and has Gene Berg crank shaft. Gene Berg features heavily in all these cars as he has the workshop and machines which make the right Volkswagen gear for easy bug handling. Back to Dave's engine, con rods are Rimco Super Rods and performance Tech cylinder heads with 44x37.5 valves help the compression ratio come out at 9.0:1. A Vertex Magneto and a pair of 48 IDA Weber carbs, Melling oil pump, Mallory Super 140 fuel pump and S&S one and three-quarter exhaust, all this helps to make a very fast motor. How about 11.48 ET at 121.17 mph at Carlsbad Race Way Park, April 1992!

Above

Speedwell BRM wheels are very rare and very expensive! Produced in England from 1966 and originally priced at £28/10s a pair. Sounds cheap now, but then it was more than a weekly wage. Speedwell was a UK company in which Graham Hill was involved. They produced many bolt-on VW performance parts in the sixties and early seventies. Graham's contact with Dan Gurney, brought an introduction to Joe Vittone, who was the founder of Engineered Motor Products Incorporated (EMPI). There was a trade swap between EMPI and Speedwell, thus wheels were sold through EMPI and EMPI parts through Speedwell. Only 30 sets exist in the world, two sets are known to be in England and the majority are in California, with the best known being on the cars of members of the DKP. One set is on Dave's car.

BUG FILE

Owner **Dave Mason**	Front suspension **Lowered**
Body mods **Stock sedan**	Rear suspension, **1968 VW**
Year **1962**	Engine **2175cc**
Wheels & tyres front **Empi BRM, Moroso**	Cam **N/a**
tyres	Ignition **Vertex Magneto**
Wheels & tyres rear **Empi BRM Firestone**	Carbs **Dual 48 IDA**
tyres	Exhaust **1 3/4 S&S**

Above

The wood-rimmed EMPI GT steering wheel is also a past time piece. Dash is all original with the exception of the large AutoMeter tach and pro light. In this model, all the seats are covered in red vinyl.

Right

You will notice that Dave has not de-chromed his bug. All the original '62 trim is in place, including the American spec overrider bumpers. Headlights are Porsche 912 items. Front brakes are stock, BRM wheels with Moroso tyres. Paint is by Danny Gabbart and is black.

All stock body at the rear except for the convertible decklid, European rear lights, BRM wheels with Firestone 6" Slicks (driven on the California streets for the photo shoot), which are attached to Berg axles and a Der Transaxle Services gearbox. '68 drums are used on the rear. The license plate surround is an Empi original. It's very rare!

BUG FILE

Owner **Greg Brinton**
Body mods **De-chromed with sunroof**
Year **1967**
Wheels &tyres front **Porsche 15x5.5**
    Kleber 145x15
Wheels & tyres rear **Porsche 15x6**
    Dunlop 205x15
Front suspension **2" drop spindle**
Rear suspension **Swing axle**
Engine **1914cc**
Cam **N/a**
Ignition **010 Bosch**
Carbs **Dual 48 ida**
Exhaust **Four tuned 1⅛" turbo muffler**

Bug number two is owned by Greg Brinton, who also races a '63 Super Street drag bug. He lives in Santa Ana and is a DKP member. Greg also works for Rimco, a leading VW engine machining company. His 1967 sunroof Sedan is no slouch either; body has been de-chromed, and painted deep black by Parker's Auto body shop in Santa Ana. The front has been lowered using 2 inch dropped spindles with Koni shocks. Porsche alloys on the front are 5x15 with Kleber 145x 15 tyres – the stance is just right! The front bumper blades are protected by EMPI bumper guards, head lights are Marchall with painted rims.

Left

Front and rear seats are stock and have been re-covered in black velour and plaid inserts. Dash is stuffed with extra gauges. In the centre is a large AutoMeter Monster Tach, which helps stop the driver from over-revving the engine. Speedo is set to the left – not as important as the rev counter! Other gauges are: VDO pyrometer ex temp, fuel, oil pressure and oil temp. EMPI leather-trimmed steering wheel and Berg locking shifter. Just to make the interior more like home, Greg installed Empi door pulls and a dash-mounted flower vase.

Above right

This is the business end of the Bug; with these guys there are no frills, merely mega horsepower. The 1914cc engine has a 69mm counterweighted crank, balanced VW con rods, VW D/P heads with 40x35.5 stainless steel valves and dual springs. Compression ratio comes out at 8.5: 1. Bosch 010 ignition, Berg 26mm oil pump and Holley fuel pump. Dual 48 IDA Webers are linked together with a Tayco linkage. After the gases have been burnt, a one-and-five-eighth inch Turbo muffler exhaust system is used to exit them.

Right

Under the '67 convertible deck lid and attached to all that horsepower is a Berg five speed gear box. Ratios are 3.78 in first, 2.06 in second, 1.58 in third, 1.21 in fourth and .89 in fifth. Rear suspension is swing axle and has drum brakes. Porsche wheels are 15x6 with Dunlop 205 65 x15, rear lights are European, (we all want the all-red American spec) and EMPI bumper guard. For added ventilation, as well as the steel sunroof, there is a pair of pop-out rear side windows.

Greg also owns this '63 drag racer that he races in Super Street. The car is stripped out and lightened ready for racing and is capable of 10.88 ET at 120mph. Displacement is 2387cc, built by Greg, with a Gene Berg 86mm crank, Carrillo rods, 94mm pistons, Engle FK89 cam. Valves are 47mm and 38mm titanium, heads are Auto Craft pro Series 910, ported and polished by Roger Crawford. Compression ratio comes out at 13.5:1. Ignition is crank-triggered and is MSD. Carbs are dual 51mm Webers, exhaust system was custom-built by Phoenix headers. The 1963 transaxle was built by Jim Kaforski at Der Transaxle Shop. Usual modifications plus others such as gusseted case, ally spool and chrome moly pinion nut. Front beam has the matching colour scheme. It has two Sway-a-ways and no caster shims but the upper control arm has been lengthened by Greg and Ray Bates. Also in the front is the spun ally gas tank, very neat and more like a street car.

Front and rear wheels are fully polished Mitchell wheels; front tyres are 15x3 M and H, and rear are 15x7 Mickey Thompson slicks. The outside of the car is Super; body work by Burrell Wilson, fibreglass work by Steve Vale, House of Colours candy and pearl paint job was done by Dick Vale, Jack Burr finished off the exterior with the lettering and art work, fake head lights.

BUG FILE

Owner **Greg Brinton**
Body mods **Glass front, de-chromed race car spec**
Year **1963**
Wheels & tyres front **Mitchell, M&H 15x3**
Wheels & tyres rear **Mitchell, Mickey Thompson 15x7 slicks**
Front suspension **Race modified two**

Sway-a-ways
Rear suspension **63 axle race modified**
Engine **2387cc**
Cam **Engle FK 87**
Ignition **Crank -trigger MSD**
Carbs **Dual Webers 51mm**
Exhaust **Custom built by Phoenix Headers**

In the early eighties when the Cal - look craze took off, some guys with original bugs decided to go for a California-style cruiser. One of the important visuals for a Cal-look bug, apart from the lowered stance and chrome wheels, was a killer paint job, so this bug was taken to Cars Etc. Huntington Beach, for a custom Coral acrylic job. Things seem to be going well, but for some reason or another, the owner did not complete the project. It was then discovered by a guy named Dyno Don, who is well known around the Californian VW scene. He bought the fifty-nine rag-top and had a friend at Marzo's upholstery shop stitch up the bug interior in grey vinyl and dark grey cloth, while the head liner was redone in white. The floor also received a grey cut loop carpet set. Bill Schwimmer, who had been into Volkswagens for some time, came across the bug at this time and Dyno, having enough unfinished projects, decided to sell. Bill, as a member of the "Der Kleiner Panzers", took it upon himself to finish the bug the way it was originally meant to be. The body and paint work was unbelievably straight and the interior was recently completed. He added the four Speedwell BRMs with Klieber 145x15 tyres on the front and Dunlop 205x65x15 tyres on the rear. The rims of the magnesium BRMs wheels were hand-polished to bring out the shine. A set of European headlights and European bumpers with EMPI bumper guards were also added.

The original 1200cc had been replaced with a 1776cc, but if you are in the "Der Kleiner Panzer" club it has to be fast. To this end, Bill and friend Marv Voegtly built a very impressive 2276cc engine from the universal 1600 case. First case was Rimco, machined for the bigger 94mm Cima pistons and a large Berg 82mm crank. At this time the case was full flowed for an external oil filter. Porsche 912 rods were used to connect the Total Seal ringed pistons to the crank and a Web Cam 86 was installed. A pair of 044 heads with welded intake ports, stainless steel valves, relocated plug holes, titanium retainers, Berg 1.45 rockers. Ignition is set up with 009 dizzy, Bosch blue coil and blue Stinger wires. Carbs are a pair of 48 Webers and exhaust is via a Phoenix one-and-five-eighth inch header into a two-and-half inch Turbo Muffler. When Dyno tested the engine, it produced 180bhp at 6000rpm this meant the standed transaxle would not last!. So Jim Kaforski at Der Transaxle built the ultimate tranny; a Rhino case type one case was used with close ratio gearing and a Gene Berg locker shifter. Also fitted were Berg axles, ZF limited slip, steel side plates, Berg trans mount and chrome axle tubes.

BUG FILE

Owner **Bill Schwimmer**

Body mods **none**

Year **1959**

Wheels & tyres front **Empi BRM Kleber 145x15**

Wheels & tyres rear **Empi BRM Dunlop 205x65x15**

Front suspension **Lowered**

Rear suspension **Stock**

Engine **2276cc**

Cam **Weber 86**

Ignition **Bosch 009**

Carbs **Dual Weber 48 IDA**

Exhaust **Phoenix 1⅝" with turbo muffler**

Interior mods include a La Carra steering wheel and custom dash with large AutoMeter Tachometer, VDO speedometer, fuel and engine hour meter. Simpson lap belts hold you in while the Sanyo AM/FM cassette deck and Pile Driver speakers, which are located behind the rear seat, try to blow you out!

HOT BITS

Above left
John Abbott dismantled the speedo on his Wizard roadster, painted the face the same colours as the interior upholstery, then fixed the main speed numbers, 30, 50 and 70mph. Note that the horn button is also colour keyed to the interior.

Left
Bill and Alison's suicide door hi-tec, Cal-look bug has a very different steering wheel. Not only is it square but it is milled out of one piece of ally; dash support is also ally. The dashboard is smoothed out and a square speedo goes with the square theme.

Above
When you completely smooth out that dashboard you have to relocate the driving instruments somewhere. Alan Smart took the RPM meter and put it under the front bulk head. Alan completely redesigned this bug in all areas as can be seen here, with the steering, brake and clutch pedal.

This may at first glance look like your standard restored cabriolet. But then it would not be hot or, as Richard King prefers to call it, 'cool'! The 1955 factory rare right hand drive cabriolet was purchased about seven years ago and has been an on and off project until late when Ritchie got down to finishing it. As with all his cars, he likes them built right, so off the floor pan came the body and some rust was found in the heater channels. With this completed, it was down to priming the body, after hours of block sanding, with the two-pack Glasurit 21 primer. Andy Barry then sprayed the shell with Glasurit BMW black, hence the time taken in the preparation stage. The floor pan was too far gone and a 1960 was purchased from John Deveroux; the pan had been fully reconditioned with new brakes and had a Hammerite paint job. To "get it down" a pair of Sway-a-ways went into the link pin beam. To help handling a Sway-a-way anti-roll bar was also fitted up front. A pair of Porsche shocks in the front and a pair of Koni shocks went in at the back and the rear was lowered by one spline. Through his business (Karmann Konnection) and trips to the USA, he came across some very nice period accessories. On the exterior are the Wolfsburg West 49- style domed hub caps on the stock steel five bolt wheels, painted light green and shod with genuine Firestone wide whites and '50s solid trims stamped with the VW logo. A pair of genuine finger plates, Porsche headlights with old head light ally eyebrows, stainless running board trims, stainless rear gravel guards and '50s chrome front, bonnet-mounted fly defector, '50s USA repro windshield trims, and Rosco mirrors. There are even more rare accessories inside.

BUG FILE

Owner **Richard King**
Body mods **Stock cabriolet**
Year **1955**
Wheels & tyres front **Stock with Firestone whitewalls**
Wheels & tyres rear **Stock with Firestone whitewalls**

Front suspension **Two Sway-a-ways**
Rear suspension **Lowered one spline**
Engine **1776cc**
Cam **N/a**
Ignition **009**
Carbs **Dual Kadrons**
Exhaust **Bug pack hide-a-way**

Left

The seats are standard and are covered in light green Sewfine covers. Sewfine also made the carpets. The steering wheel is a VDM accessory with a compass horn push which is very rare. Added to the VDM is a full circle horn ring. Behind the wheel is a SWF turn signal lever with headlight flasher. The original dash grille has been replaced with a Perahaus eight day wind-up clock and grille. Clipped to the grill is a Rosenthall bud vase, that Ritchie picked up in the USA. Other rare items are the locking glove compartment and above this is a grab handle – another accessory. These were not fitted to Beetles as standard until 1959. A rare bambus parcel shelf is under the dashboard and just gives that finishing touch.

Above

A 1776cc motor came from Mark at the German Car Company. A pair of Kadron carbs went onto the fully ported heads. The heads have stainless steel valves, crank is stock and so are the con rods. Oiling is achieved with a Melling pump, ignition is 009 dizzy with blue coil, exhaust is Bugpack hideaway. Electrics are now 12 volt, and it really flies.

BUG FILE

Owner **June Key**	Front suspension **Lowered 2" Golf struts**
Body mods **Stock cabriolet**	Rear suspension **Stock**
Year **1974**	Engine **1776cc**
Wheels & tyres front **Stock Bridgestone**	Cam **Stock**
165x15	Ignition **009**
Wheels & tyres rear **Stock Bridgestone**	Carbs **Dual 48 Dellortos**
165x15	Exhaust **Stock**

Right

This is our own cabriolet – June and myself bought it from an American who had driven it into the front of a tractor! While rebuilding the front a friend, Paul Wayling and myself turned it into a right hand drive. We replaced the front of the car including the dash and inner fender panels. The floor pan was also replaced with a right hand drive pan. Front struts are Golf with stock 1303 springs. To lower the front a little, a friend, Trevor Chinn and myself also fitted a Passat rack and pinion steering. All the original parts were put back on or replaced. This makes the cabriolet look stock but the interior and motor have been modified. Paint is E-type Jaguar primrose yellow.

Above

The basic 1600 case was machined and modified to feed an external oil filter. Into the case went a counterweighted and balanced 69mm crank with stock rods. 90mm barrels and pistons were next and above these went a pair of new heads with stainless valves; the stock cam was also retained. A pair of Dellorto carbs really liven up the performance. Front seats are from an Audi, they are installed on the 1303 runner system, rear seat is stock as is most of the rest of the interior, seats and door panels are covered in mid-grey Connolly leather by Bob Wells of Mildenhall.

Above left

The brilliant Porsche magenta paint and the polished Porsche 911 wheels grab your attention with this super Wizard roadster. Built as a body off project by Andy Pearce, the floor pan was strengthened before the roof was cut off and the body mods were also done at this point. The base car was a '67 Swedish import, hence left hand drive; a car from this year also has the advantage of front disc brakes; Type Three brakes were fitted to the rear. The bug has been lowered, five to six inches, Sway-a-ways on the front and two splines on the rear and fitted with a chrome anti-roll bar for looks and to improve handling.

Headlights are Rossi with built-in turn indicators, a chrome "towel rail" type nerf bar gives front protection. The Wizard is now owned by Terry and Sue Gordon.

Left

Rear deck lid has been removed to show the 1641cc engine, colour keyed to the body colour and chrome plated for show. This engine was built from the original 1500cc case with standard crank, con rods, heads, and fitted with stainless steel valves and 009 dizzy. A Melling oil pump and electric Facet fuel pump feed the twin Weber 34ICT carbs. Exhaust is a big bore with taper tips. Gear box is from a GT beetle to improve the ratios (especially on motorways). Rear lights are 1939 Ford tear-drops

Above

The two plus two interior features a milled ally panel from the USA, housing the original speedo and VDO gauges. The roll bar is from a Beach Buggy manufacturer and was cut to fit neatly into the Wizard body, but low enough not to interfere with the roadster's lines painted the body colour. Front seats are Ford XR2 recovered in two different grey cloths and the rear seat was made to fit. Steering wheel is an Asztrali four spoke.

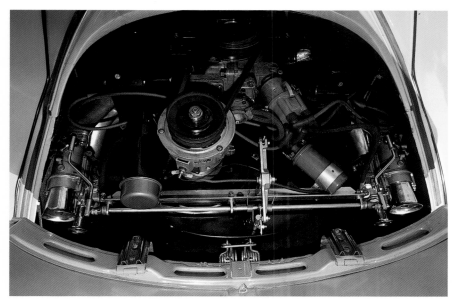

Left

Here is another California Looker, in the old style, built by Brody Hoyt. Brody works for the great VW master Gene Berg – so you would not expect anything other than a real 'hot bug'. The 1965 sedan has no body mods, one-piece windows and Cal-look window rubbers. All the trim is intact and looks good. Headlights are American spec, turn indicators are also original, but look at the stance; it is just right. Front beam is adjustable and is also equipped with caster shims. The body was painted by Brody and Russell Gate and the colour is Weathercliffe pearl orange.

Above

This is the real 'hot' bit of this bug! Capacity is a huge 1995cc which is achieved with: a welded 82mm crankshaft, Gene Berg 5.400 con rods, Clyde Berg cylinder heads with 40x37.5 Manley stainless steel valves (compression ratio is 7.3:1), Bosch 009 dizzy. A stock fuel pump feeds the twin 48 IDA Weber carbs. A 30mm Gene Berg oil pump feeds the oil into a Berg oil filter and a three-and-a-half quart sump. Exhaust is fed out by a Gene Berg one-and-five-eighth inch system. The gearbox was built by Gary Berg and runs stock gears with welded third and fourth a poor man's posi and a beef-a-diff, all Gene Berg.

BUG FILE

Owner **Brody Hoyt**	Front suspension **Adjustable**
Body mods **One-piece**	**front beam**
windows	Rear suspension **Swing axle**
Year **1965**	Engine **1995cc**
Wheels & tyres front **911**	Cam **N/a**
Porsche Kleber 135x15	Ignition **Bosch 009**
Wheels 8 tyres rear **911**	Carbs **Dual Weber 48 IDA**
Porsche, summit 165x15	Exhaust **Gene Berg 1⅝"**

Left

The dash is left stock, steering wheel is a LaCarra, shifter is a Gene Berg. The front seats are from a Honda Prelude and covered in cord velour; door panels are also covered.

Above

All stock body, original rear lights, American spec, all red. Wheels are original Porsche 911, six inch front and rear, front tyres are 135x15 Kleber and 165x15 Summit on the rear.

BUG FILE

Owner **Ted & Jason Stevens**
Year **1955**
Body mods **De-chromed
     louvers, frenched aerial**
Wheels & tyres front **Boyd, Bridgestone
     tyres**
Wheels & tyres rear **Boyd. Bridgestone
     tyres**
Front suspension **Lowered**
Rear suspension **1971**
Engine **1700cc**
Cam **4063 bugpack**
Ignition **Vertex Magneto**
Carbs **Dual Weber 40 idf**
Exhaust **S&S header**

The 'hot bug' bug is all over the world. This bug was built by a father and son team in Duncan, British Columbia, Canada. Having built show cars in the past for other people, Ted and Jason Stevens of GT Collision, decided to build their own. The attention to detail on this car is top class. The '55 oval body had all the seams welded and smoothed to give the clean look. The pan was given the same amount of detailing; it was welded and moulded and then given five coats of Imron magenta paint. Sikkens black paint was shot on the body by Lester at GT Collision. After Ted and Jason had finished the body and pan. They applied the pink and blue graphics. Adjusters were used to lower the front and the spring plates on the rear. Wheels are Boyds and are wrapped in Bridgestone Potenza tyres. Disc brakes on all four corners are chrome plated as are the shocks, front trailing arms, sway bar, axle tubes, spring plates. Other components include polished ally items such as Briz front and rear bumpers and engine hardware. Headlights are Rossis.

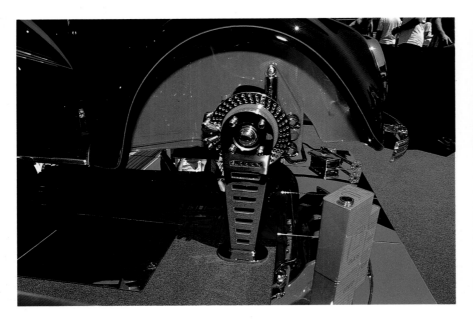

Above

This is detailing! Under wings are smoothed and painted Imron magenta – as good as the body! Chrome discs, shocks and trailing arms. A billett ally stand and mirrors help show the finish on the floor pan.

Right

The 1700cc engine was built by Peter Robert of Sooke, Canada. A counterweighted 69mm crank, reworked stock rods, Bug pack 4063 camshaft, Cima 88mm pistons and barrels with dual port heads with Manley SS valves. This gives a 9.25:1 compression ratio. A pair of dual Weber 40 IDF carbs are actuated by a Tayco linkage, a Vertex magneto and Mallory wires fire the gases. Fire wall is stainless with a ribbed fan-like pattern. Fan housing is painted with graphics; if it is not painted it is chromed. The billett ally rocker covers and pulleys etc. are polished.

BUG FILE

Owner **Bill Newton**
Year **1969**
Body mods **Baja**
Wheels & tyres front **Pro comp series 12s, 245x60x14**
Wheels & tyres rear **Pro comp series 12s, 265x60x15**
Front suspension **Stock**
Rear suspension **69 IRS**
Engine **1955cc**
Cam **Engle 110**
Ignition **009**
Carbs **Dual 48 DRLA Dellortos**
Exhaust **Chromed megaphones**

This radical show-winning Baja was built by Bill Newton, the 'Bug' doctor, from Louisville, Kentucky. The body and paint were done by Carl Spalding at Carl's Customotive in Louisville. A fibreglass baja bug kit from Johnny's Speed and Chrome went on first. The wings were moulded to the body. Chevrolet Vega rear lights, rectangular head-lights and the aerial were frenched into the wings and body. A set of one-piece windows were also installed in the doors. The pan was smoothed out with a 16swg hand-rolled steel belly pan. Under the fenders and fire wall were also smoothed out. Coats of Polyester primer were hand-rubbed and a gloss black guide coat was used to check before final painting. Base coat of white for the bright colours and dark charcoal base for the violet metal flake, graphics are done in cherry pink, mustard yellow, organic blue and tangerine orange. Four coats of clear went on top and then colour sanded.

Above

An open weave cloth was used by Billy Scott to cover the dash, door panels, seats, headliner and floor. They were then stitched in lavender vinyl and red piping for accents. Front seats are cut down '83 Datsun highbacks and the matching rear seats were made by Billy Scott. A hot pink Formuling France steering wheel and Stewart-Warner custom gauges; Hurst supplied the shifter. Other interior tricks include AM/FM cassette deck, panasonic TV and Cellular phone.

Right

The blueprinted and balanced 1955cc engine has a Berg 76mm counterweighted and eight doweled crankshaft, stock VW rods, Cima 90.5mm pistons and Engle 110 cam. Bill ported and polished the dual port heads and installed 40x35.5mm Manley stainless steel valves. A pair of 48 Dellorto carbs and a Bosch 009 dizzy fire the engine and exhaust gases exit through a pair of chrome megaphone headers.

This '71 super Beetle convertible was built by Sean Cour, it was purchased from the brother of Sean's boss at Jerry's Custom Paint in Portland, Oregon. This is a body-off rebuild and when the body and pan were split Mike Geiszler at Jerry's Custom Paint filled all the spot welds and assembly-line flaws. The body was then taken to a street rod shop, Restorations and Reproductions, where the owner Mike McKent shaved the turn signals, taillights, door handles, gas filler door and de-chromed the body. The exhaust cut-outs in the rear valance were also filled. Mike also cut out and filled the stock dash and replaced it with a raised steel one. After the pan had been smoothed out it also went to Restorations and Reproductions where a removable full ally belly pan was fitted, secured by 48 stainless machine screws. Sean and Ron Morfitt, head painter at Jerry's, finished preparing the body and Ron then laid on the Sikkens black urethane (with a touch of blue pearl), and covered the base with Sikkens clear. Next came the graphics. Mitch Kim took some time in designing, taping and spraying; 80 hours of taping, 30 hours of airbrushing work. The pan was first, then the body, and in places where it is not usually seen. Wheels are Boyds, polished 15x6, with 195x50 fronts and 205x60 rears. Front struts are adjustable with cut coils. Front brakes are Karmann Ghia and the rears are Porsche 914. Front and rear bumpers are Briz three-ribbed ally.

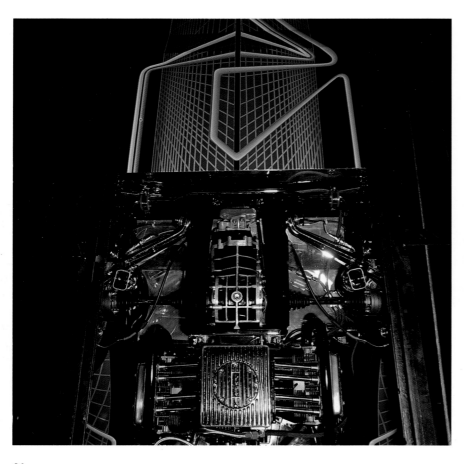

Above

Gearbox/trans axle and the lower half of the engine have been detailed as well as the rest of the car. The belly pan has also been painted and carries the graphic design; what has not been chromed or polished has been painted.

Right

Sean built up the turbocharged 1641cc engine. He managed to complete it using all the right bits! Cima 87mm pistons, Engle 110 cam, 041 heads with minor porting and polishing, dual Dellorto 40mm DRLA carbs and a blow-through turbo from CB performance. There is also a host of billett ally accessories. The graphics on the fan housing are a small copy of the rest of the car.

*Custom dash has the same graphic
design and houses a range of Stewart-
Warner Track Force gauges, Momo Air
leather steering wheel. Front seats are
Cerullo and covered in grey velour as are
the rear seats and the door panels. A
custom ally console under the dash
houses the Sony AM/FM disc player and
Rockford Fosgate PA-1 equaliser.*

Above

A pair of USA spec headlights in the sloped front fenders which also house the front turn indicators with repeaters on the side of the body. The front beam has been cut and turned and the rear has been lowered one and a half inches. This makes the car sit well and still gives a good ride with the original shocks. One-piece windows and a de-chrome, plus shaving the trunk and deck lid handles complete the smooth look. Painted and polished five spoke Empis with Goodyear rubber look just right.

Above right

Most of the interior was taken from a Ford XR3i. This includes both front and rear seats. A Kenwood stereo head unit is in the now panelled glove compartment and a CD player is under the rear seat. These run into a Pioneer 180 watt amplifier with the speakers on the back shelf. A new head liner was installed along with the black cloth-covered door panels and carpets. The neat wood rimmed steering wheel is a Dino classic and Mads repainted the speedo yellow.

Right

A stock 1200cc engine sits in an ally fire-walled bay. The fan housing, air filter and tin ware are painted yellow and silver, with a little chrome. Very clean and effective.

BUG FILE

Owner **Mads Moller Nielsen**
Year **1960**
Body mods **1951 split window, de-chrome, one-piece windows**
Wheels & tyres front **5 spoke empi, Goodyear**
Wheels & tyres rear **5 spoke empi, Goodyear**
Front suspension **Cut and turned.**
Rear suspension **Lowered 1½"**
Engine **1200cc**
Can **Stock**
Ignition **Stock**
Carb **Stock**
Exhaust **Transporter pipe**

What can you do if you have scoured Denmark for a Split rear window Beetle and you have not been able to find one, but during your searching you find a real 'rotten up to the waist' 1951 with a good roof and the Split rear window intact and in good shape? The answer is: you locate a 1960, with which you do a roof transplant. This is what Mads Nielsen of Copenhagen and a member of The Copenhagen Aircoolers carried out, and succeeded with this Ginster Yellow cal-looker. The floor pan was blasted and then painted black metallic. With the body back on the pan the Britax sun roof was installed next and then the roof was cut behind the sunroof and down to the deck lid, complete with window and air intake. Easy! not really; there is a lot of body work to make it look original. To finish off the Split look, a pair of small Oval rear lights and a Pope's nose number plate light on an original 'W' deck lid were fitted.